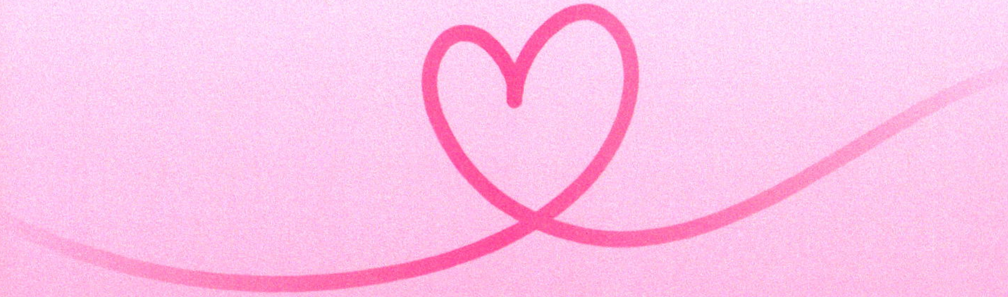

Dedication

To my Mum and Grandma.

In life, you gave us endless love and support.

In death, you are providing wisdom, strength and courage to your continued feminine line.

Always loved and by our sides.

For this we honour and thank you.

All rights reserved.
No part of this book may be reproduced by any
mechanical, photographic, or electronic process,
or in the form of a photographical recording,
nor may it stored in a retrieval system, transmitted
or otherwise be copied for public or private use
other than for fair use as brief quotations embodied
in articles and reviews without expressed written
permission of the publisher.

This journal was channelled from my Light team
and my own Higher self to help you heal your Soul.
It should not, however, under any circumstances,
be substituted for professional medical advice,
nor does this author prescribe the use of any technique
as a form of treatment in lieu of medical treatment
given for or by medical professionals.

This Journal is an accompaniment to such
medical treatment prescribed by a medical professional
to aid your emotional, mental, physical and spiritual
well-being. In the event you use any of the information
in this book for yourself, the author and the publisher
assume no responsibility for your actions and
is at the reader's discretion and risk.

ISBN Number: 978-1-7392936-1-1
Publisher: Jo Wesch, jowesch.com
Copyright Ownership: Jo Wesch 2024
This Journal is part of LOVE YOUR AURA®

Acknowledgements

Firstly to my Light team, thank you for being
my guiding light and divine support.

Without you, I would not have been able to
channel and publish this journal.

To my earthly support network, I humbly thank you
from the bottom of my heart.

Lynne Stainthorpe who was her normal kind and patient self,
for editing and ensuring I was on-point and brand, her
techie guru Nick for ensuring it was in the correct format
for printing and my beta testers, Poppy, Nicky, Dolly, Liz and
Susan. I really appreciated you taking the time in telling me
what you liked and more importantly what you didn't.

My loving family, who are all so special to me.

Without these wonderful beings
this journal would not have been created.

Dearest beautiful Soul

Welcome to this journal about you.

How you feel about you, and how you would like others and the Universe to treat and view you.

This will be an insightful healing journey, one you may wish to re-travel over different parts of your life.

Important things to note about this journal:

1. The more honest you are with yourself, the more you will heal.

2. Some elements may be too hard to answer straight away and that is OK, please do not ever be upset if there are elements that are just too raw. Leave them and come back when you feel you are ready.

3. This is your journal so do what you wish. Draw pictures, doodle, and write. Let your creativity flow. Don't feel guilty about how you express yourself as long as you are honest with yourself.

4. This is for you alone.

5. Enjoy.

With love & blessings,

Jo x

Love yourself, make peace with yourself, that's the first step to being able to live life in peace.

Anon

Contents

ONE: A Letter to Your Soul 13

TWO: If Only I Had the Time 23

THREE: Planting the Seeds for your Future 35

FOUR: 7-day Grateful Journalling 59

FIVE: Your 7-day Guide to Shadow Love 77

SIX: Forgiveness 95

SEVEN: The Gift of Thank You 105

EIGHT: I Am 119

NINE: Finding your Voice 153

TEN: Reflections of the Soul 163

"Today, I release the shackles of my past to allow the shoots of tomorrow to flourish."

Jo Wesch, The Aura Healer

ONE

A Letter to Your Soul

Asking your Soul for help

Asking your soul for help

I would like you to write to your higher self asking for its help for whatever your inner self needs right now.

I fully appreciate that it won't be easy. Yet if you are wholly honest with your Soul, the Universe will know how to help you as you have been brave enough to ask for it.

Write it as if you were looking into the mirror of your Soul and asking what do I need?

"Find room
in your heart
for the things that
mean the most to you."

Jo Wesch, The Aura Healer

TWO

If Only I Had the Time

Appreciating the importance of time

What's most important for you right now, during the week?

In the Ferris wheel of life, time is the biggest restrictor there is. In your life currently, where do each of the following rank for the amount of time you spend?

- Family?
- Work/school?
- Chores?
- Me time?
- Sleep?

Add in any additional areas you wish:

-
-
-
-
-

What's most important for you right now, during the week?

From your list, what has become routine and what has become an excuse for not finding the time?

If life didn't get in the way, what would be the biggest change you could make?

What would be the smallest change that you could easily make right now?

THREE

Planting the Seeds for Your Future

Allowing limitless possibilities into your life

Planting the seeds for your future

If you were given seeds to plant for your future, what would they be?

The sky is the limit, use your imagination and be creative.

Over the 5 days plant an idea, a dream, or a wish.

Things that you would like to add to your life daily, weekly, monthly, or even less frequently. In time, see which ones have come to fruition for telling the Universe your dreams.

Nothing is that easy, I hear you say. No, it's not, I agree, but if there were no limits to your wishes and dreams, what would you remove from your life to make room for these?

To allow you more space I have given each day 3 pages of pots, so fill them well, and try not to limit them to material items, remember your emotions and traits which you wish you have more of e.g. confidence, love, etc.

Every day you will have a page to declutter your life. Let's call it weeding, just like you would do in a garden.

Day 1:
The first plant pot is for the occasional things that you would like to undertake.

The second plant pots are
for the seeds that are needed
or wanted monthly.

The third set of pots is for everyday
requirements that you would like
to grow in your life.

Things that you are going to declutter or get rid of in your life to allow room for your dreams and wishes:

Day 2:
The first plant pot is for the occasional things that you would like to undertake.

The second plant pots are
for the seeds that are needed
or wanted monthly.

The third set of pots is for everyday requirements that you would like to grow in your life.

Things that you are going to declutter or get rid of in your life to allow room for your dreams and wishes:

Day 3:
The first plant pot is for the occasional things that you would like to undertake.

The second plant pots are
for the seeds that are needed
or wanted monthly.

The third set of pots is for everyday requirements that you would like to grow in your life.

Things that you are going to declutter or get rid of in your life to allow room for your dreams and wishes:

Day 4:
The first plant pot is for the occasional things that you would like to undertake.

The second plant pots are
for the seeds that are needed
or wanted monthly.

The third set of pots is for everyday requirements that you would like to grow in your life.

Things that you are going to declutter or get rid of in your life to allow room for your dreams and wishes:

Day 5:
The first plant pot is for the occasional things that you would like to undertake.

The second plant pots are
for the seeds that are needed
or wanted monthly.

The third set of pots is for everyday requirements that you would like to grow in your life.

How easy or difficult was this exercise?
Was it easier to declutter or
to plant for the future?

"Gratitude makes what you have into enough."

Lynne Stainthorpe

FOUR

7-day Grateful Journalling

What are you grateful for?

Dearest beautiful Soul

This section is about remembering the grace and beauty in your life and being grateful for it. This may be remembering what you once had, or what you currently have in your life now.

However, without these people or experiences, your life would not have been so whole. For example, you may be grateful for someone who has passed on but left a special place in your heart.

You may be grateful for certain elements that hold material value (such as your home); others, may not cost anything at all from a financial perspective. These are the ones that hold a special place in your heart and may be linked to relationships with other people.

So, reach into your heart and ask yourself the following:

- If I did not have a certain person in my life, how different would it have been?

- If I had not experienced a certain situation in my life, how different could my life have been?

- Would I miss my prized possession if it was gone?

- What are the little things in life that keep me grateful and blessed, knowing that without these little things, life on a bad day would not feel as good?

In this section, I have given 7 days of different opportunities to journal. Remember, this is your Journal so whatever you write is right for you and nobody will judge you.

Blessed be,

Jo x

Day 1:
Today I am grateful for...

Day 2:
Today I am grateful for...

Day 3:
Today I am grateful for...

Day 4:
Today I am grateful for...

Day 5:
Today I am grateful for...

Day 6:
Today I am grateful for...

Day 7:
Today I am grateful for...

FIVE

Your 7-day Guide to Shadow Love

Learning to love the whole of you

Every day should be a Shadow Love Day

Which areas of your life are you too hard on yourself?

Do you ever feel like you are not worthy or enough for some reason?

I would like to start by saying that you are enough.
More than enough, you are amazing!

Now what will it take for you to believe this?

This is the 7-day Shadow Love part of the journal.
The purpose is to shine a light on those areas of your life that you prefer to remain hidden. These areas truly deserve your love and respect so that you can be whole.

I appreciate this section will not be easy, yet truly loving the whole of you is what this journal is all about.

Best of luck,

Jo x

Day 1: Shadow Love

Day 2: Shadow Love

Day 3: Shadow Love

Day 4: Shadow Love

Day 5: Shadow Love

Day 6: Shadow Love

Day 7: Shadow Love

SIX

Forgiveness

The gift of forgiving yourself

Forgiving yourself for past mistakes is one of the hardest lessons you can learn

Make a note of the times in your life that you may have buried because they were just too painful or traumatic.

This section is intended to allow yourself the forgiveness, comfort, and release you truly deserve.

Whether this was caused by the hand of another, or you caused a misdeed and felt unworthy of forgiveness, now is the time to release and move forward.

Then think about the Hawaiian forgiveness prayer "Ho'opnonpono".

*I am sorry,
Please forgive me.
Thank you,
I love you.*

These words are most powerful when you say them aloud to yourself. Give yourself forgiveness for these past misdeeds by journalling how each one makes you feel. Then picture each note returning to dust and back to the Universe.

Give yourself the freedom and love to truly forgive yourself.

FORGIVE
yourself

FORGIVE
yourself

FORGIVE
yourself

SEVEN

The Gift of Thank You

Accepting them as a gift from the heart

Words have started wars, so why can't they be used to heal?

When you receive a compliment, how do you react?

If someone says "Thank you" to you, how do you receive it? Do you say, "Oh, it was nothing", "Oh you are most welcome" or "You are most welcome, I appreciate you saying that"?

If you receive a physical gift that you can materially see, it makes you feel happy. By retraining your mind to accept compliments in the same way as a material gift, it will show to the Universe that you can receive gifts of love and thanks in the joy of words.

So the next set of pages are for each compliment that you receive. Write how each of them makes you feel, how you received the compliment, and the next time you receive one how you would like to feel after receiving it.

You will note that this is not a 7-day's worth, so whenever you receive a compliment just add it, and then journal about it.

I am going to be the first, let's see how you take it…

"You are an amazing Soul"

NO WORRIES
HAVE A GOOD DAY!
NEW IDEAS
BELIEVE & ACHIEVE
SMILE PLEASE
REMEMBER EVERYTHING WILL BE FINE
YOU CAN DO IT
LOVE YOURSELF

EIGHT

Affirmations

Make today an "I am" …… day

Here is a section on positive affirmations. We all need them in our life, no matter how strong we are.

Believing in them, however, is something far harder.

Write down how each of them makes you feel.
Alternatively, add to the sentence to bring more into your life,
e.g. "I am worthy" could also be "I am worthy of love and respect".
Do not limit yourself.

Grab yourself some post-it notes and write on each of
them what you wrote within this journal. Stick them on a mirror
and say them aloud each day for a week.

Afterwards, write down how you feel about the words now.

I have also added pages for you to add your own affirmations,
ensure that each one is positive and unapologetic of who
you want to be. It doesn't matter if you are not there yet,
you are striving for it.

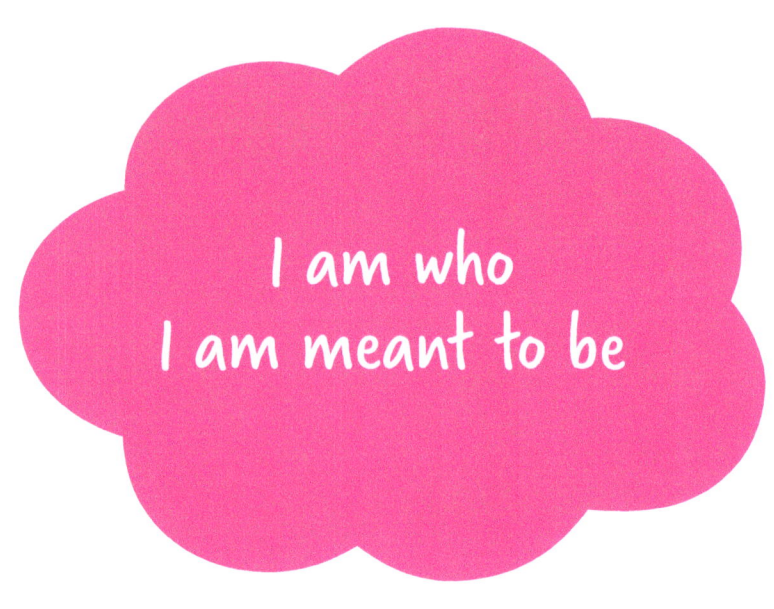

Your Voice Matters

NINE

Finding Your Voice

Allowing your voice to be heard without apologies

Over time, people have been told what to say and when to say it

Think of Nelson Mandela, who received a 27 year jail sentence for his beliefs and words.

During Covid-19, you had to wear a mask and this suppressed your voice.

"You should be seen and not heard" was often a thing a child might have heard or described how you should behave.

Well, this section is unapologetically "your voice" and you are not to be suppressed in anything you wish to say.

Be bold, be proud, and unapologetically you.

Below are a few of my favourite quotes from Nelson Mandela to inspire you:

"A winner is a dreamer who never gives up."

"I learned that courage was not the absence of fear, but the triumph over it. The brave man is not he who does not feel afraid, but he who conquers that fear."

"Live life like nobody is watching, and express yourself like the whole world is listening."

TEN

Reflections of the Soul

A thank you to your Soul

At the beginning of this journal, I asked you to write a letter to your Soul asking for its help

Now I want you to write a Thank You letter to your Soul, reflecting upon what you have learned through this journal.

The words are yours.

Own them and stand in your power to deliver them.

Be bold, be proud, and unapologetically you.

Dearest beautiful Soul

I want to thank you from the bottom of my heart for purchasing this journal, which I hope was both cathartic and healing.

Whilst I appreciate that certain elements may have been very hard for you to put pen to paper, I think you really ought to give yourself a well-deserved pat on the back for the bravery it took to be so open and honest.

I wanted to share with you how the idea for this journal came about. As my bio states, I am an Aura Healer – your aura consists of energetic fields that surround your body – and my Spirit Guides provided me with certain topics which they felt would be helpful for people to have within one journal. And so The Heart of Your Soul was created.

Like you, I have lived, cried, released the pain, and healed through writing this journal, and I now feel that I have also grown from what I have shared.

I would love to hear back from you on your experiences with the Journal, so, why not drop me an email at journal@jowesch.com

Love & blessings,

About the Author

Jo is an Aura Healer and mystic who has spent many years
undertaking Inner Soul work to create the person she is today.

Working intuitively with her Spirit guides, she brings you
creative healing tools such as this Self-love Journal,
to enable you to start your healing process.

For more information about what Jo does,
why not visit her on Facebook or on her website.

Facebook: Jo Wesch, the Aura Healer
Email: journal@jowesch.com
jowesch.com

www.ingramcontent.com/pod-product-compliance
Lightning Source LLC
Chambersburg PA
CBHW061146170426
43209CB00011B/1569